START-UP
GEOGRAPHY

TRAFFIC AND SAFETY

Anna Lee

Evans

Published by Evans Brothers Limited
2A Portman Mansions
Chiltern Street
London W1U 6NR

© Evans Brothers Limited 2003
Reprinted 2004, 2005
Produced for Evans Brothers Limited by
White-Thomson Publishing Ltd.
2/3 St Andrew's Place
Lewes, East Sussex BN7 1UP

Printed in China by W K T Co. Ltd.

Editor: Elaine Fuoco-Lang
Consultants: Lorraine Harrison, Senior Lecturer in
Geography Education at the University of Brighton
and Christine Bentall, Key Stage One teacher at
St Bartholomew's Church of England Primary
School, Brighton.
Designer: Tessa Barwick
Map artwork: The Map Studio

Cover: All photographs by Alan Towse

British Library Cataloguing in Publication Data
Lee, Anna
   Traffic and safety. - (Start-up geography)
   1.Traffic safety - Juvenile literature
   I.Title
   363.1'25
ISBN: 0 237 52460 0

Acknowledgements
The publishers would like to thank staff, students and
parents at St Bartholemew's C.E. Primary School,
Brighton, for their involvement in the preparation of
this book.

Picture Acknowledgements:
All photographs by Alan Towse except Robert Picket
11.

Contents

Our school

▼ Our school is on the corner of a quiet street and a busy street in the centre of a big city.

There are many traffic controls in our local area.

centre city traffic controls

▶ **Some control traffic on the road ...**

◀ **... some control where people park their cars ...**

▶ **... and some make roads safe for pedestrians.**

park   pedestrians

The roads we live in

▶ There are many shops near Eshna's house.

Her street is busy during the day, when the shops are open.

◀ Janet's street is busiest in the evenings.

She lives in an area where there are lots of cafés.

busy busiest area

Most of the people who drive down
Louis' street live there.
It is a no-through road.
No-through roads are usually quiet.

Which streets are busy in your local area?
Do you know why?

drive   no-through road   quiet   7

Rush hour

Many people drive to work or catch the bus.

Most people travel to and from work at the same time.

Most people start work at about 9 a.m. and finish at about 5 p.m.

travel

Traffic on many
roads is very heavy in
the morning and evening.

These times are called 'rush hour'.
Sometimes there are traffic jams in rush hour.

very heavy   rush hour   traffic jams   9

Traffic controls

Traffic controls help prevent traffic jams and accidents.

How do the signs on this page control traffic?

STOP

30

BUS LANE

LOOK BOTH WAYS

No Waiting
No Loading
No Parking

At any time

WARNING

One way

prevent   accidents   signs

There are different types of traffic controls on motorways.

People use motorways to drive long distances.

For 24 miles

Slow vehicles aren't allowed on motorways.

This helps to keep the traffic moving.

motorways   distances   vehicles   **11**

Making roads safer

There are many ways to make roads safer.

▼ Speed humps make cars drive more slowly.

► Pedestrian areas are places for people to walk. Traffic is not allowed.

safer speed humps slowly

▲ **Fencing stops small children running into the road.**

► **Cycleways keep cyclists away from other traffic.**

What traffic controls near your school make roads safer?

fencing   cycleways

Pedestrian safety

▼ **Traffic lights** **by our school make the road safer for pedestrians.**

▶ **Street signs** **warn drivers to watch out for children.**

traffic lights warn

We don't have a zebra crossing. Our lollipop lady helps us cross the road.

We wrote to the local council to ask them to make a zebra crossing for our school.

Brighton & Hove

ST BARTHOLOMEW'S
C.E. PRIMARY SCHOOL

Ann Street
Brighton
BN1 4GP

23rd June

Dear Sir/Madam

Our class has been finding out about traffic in our local area. We would like to have a zebra crossing outside our school. This would help us to cross the road safely.

Please could you tell us if this is possible?

Yours faithfully

Year two class
St Bartholomew's Primary School

Telephone/Fax (01273) 692463
Head Teacher: Mrs A L Page, MA

zebra crossing   lollipop lady

Parking controls

It can be difficult to find a place to park in our town.

There are places where **drivers** are allowed to park ...

drivers

... and places where parking is not allowed.

No Waiting
No Loading
At any time   No Parking

WARNING

What do the different controls on these pages mean?

Our traffic survey

We conducted a survey on traffic to find out when the street near our school is busiest.

To make it fair we counted the number of cars in the street at the same time each day for four days.

conducted survey fair

Here are our results.

Traffic survey for New England Street, Brighton			
	Monday	Tuesday	Wednesday
9.30 a.m.–9.40 a.m.	21	17	19
12.30 p.m.–12.40 p.m.	16	13	10
3.00 p.m.–3.10 p.m.	25	28	21

On which day was New England Street busiest?

What time of day is usually the quietest?

results   quietest

Traffic and parking

Here is a map of the area around our school.

The different parking and traffic controls nearby are all marked.

Can you say what each control is for?

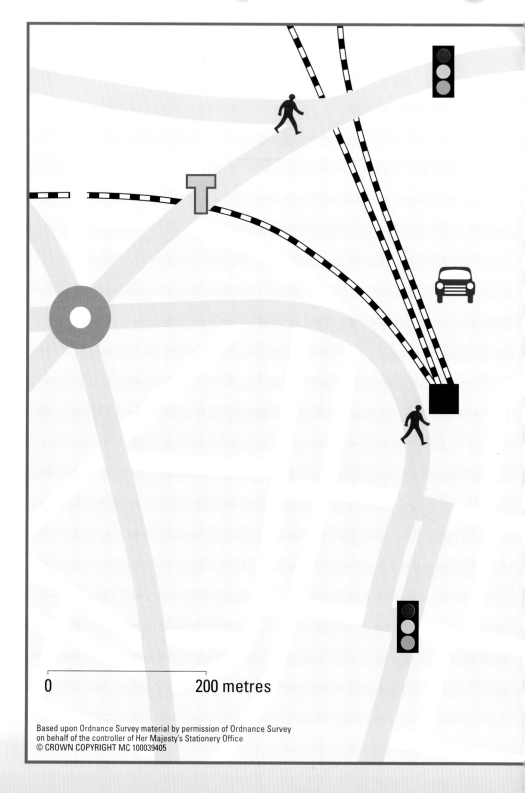

0   200 metres

controls in our area

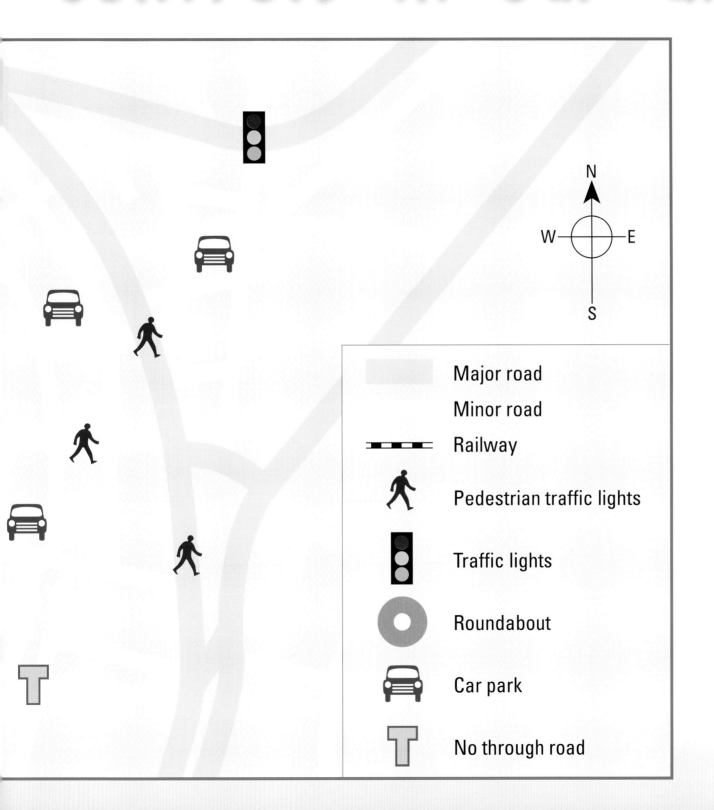

Major road

Minor road

Railway

Pedestrian traffic lights

Traffic lights

Roundabout

Car park

No through road

Further information for

Possible Activities

SPREAD ONE

Create a 3D or 2D map of the area round the school highlighting traffic controls.

Describe how many different ways you can park 6 cars.

How many other warning signs can the children think of e.g. animal signs?

SPREAD TWO

Identify the different kinds of roads the pupils live in.

SPREAD THREE

Conduct a survey to find out about how parents/carers/adults who work at school get to work. Do they experience traffic jams? Are there alternative ways of travelling?

SPREAD FOUR

Use a camera to photograph traffic controls around the school. Plot these onto a street plan. Ask the children to consider different kinds of controls that could be added to make the area safer/quieter.

What shapes and colours are used to make signs and what do they mean?

Slow vehicles are not allowed on motorways. Can the children think of any slow vehicles that may not be allowed on motorways?

SPREAD FIVE

Carry out a small project of the local area to find out how our roads could be made safer. Look at a local area and ask the children to write a letter to the local council with the findings and suggest any improvements.

Parents and Teachers

SPREAD SIX

Find out how pedestrians use the local area and use this information to write a newspaper report. Include a range of evidence such as photographs, plans or picture maps, interviews with local residents etc.

Practise the green cross code for roads that do not have special places (e.g. traffic lights or zebra crossings) to cross.

SPREAD SEVEN

Look at the different parking controls in the local area. Create a 2D map of the area and draw on the different controls.

Make a multi-storey car park using boxes.

SPREAD EIGHT

Conduct your own traffic survey and draw a graph to show the busiest and quietest times. How do the results compare with the one in the book? Also specify different types of vehicles.

SPREAD NINE

Ask the children to describe a journey they regularly take, thinking of the different traffic and parking controls they come across.

Have a brainstorming session and think of as many traffic and parking controls as you can.

Make traffic signs to use in the playground. Draw roads on the playground in chalk and divide the class up into vehicles and pedestrians.

Further Information

BOOKS

FOR CHILDREN

Schools by Sally Hewitt (Franklin Watts 2000)
Street by Sally Hewitt (Franklin Watts 2000)
Travelling About by Sally Hewitt (Franklin Watts 2000)
Where We Live by Sally Hewitt (Franklin Watts 2000)
School by Jeff Stanfield (Hodder Wayland 1999)
The Street by Jeff Stanfield (Hodder Wayland 1999)

FOR ADULTS

Handbook of Primary Geography by Roger Carter (Ed) (The Geographical Association 1998)

Also refer to the Green Cross Code, The Highway Code (Road Safety Directorate/Driving Standards Agency 2001) and *A Safer Journey to School* (DfEE Publications)

WEBSITES

http://www.local-transport.dft.gov.uk/schooltravel/safe/index.htm
http://www.standards.dfee.gov.uk/schemes/geography
http://www.streetmap.co.uk
http://www.learn.co.uk
http://www.schoolzone.co.uk
http://www.roads.detr.gov.uk/roadsafety/index.htm

Index